THE
DECOUPAGE
GALLERY

THE
DECOUPAGE GALLERY

A COLLECTION OF OVER 450 COLOR

AND 550 BLACK-AND-WHITE

DESIGN MOTIFS

DEE DAVIS and GAIL B. COOPER

WATSON-GUPTILL PUBLICATIONS/NEW YORK

ACKNOWLEDGMENTS

We very much appreciate the permission given by Pollock's Toy Museum in London to reproduce the pictures from *Pollock's World of Toys* and *The Rainy Day Book*.

We would like to acknowledge and thank our friends William Konecky, for permission to reproduce the two Redouté prints, *Gloxinie* and *Tulipe de Gesner* on page 35; and Lois Silberman for permission to reproduce a part of her collection of cigar labels on pages 65, 67, and 69.

Thank you also to our wonderful designer, Areta Buk, for her creativity; to our patient editor, Alisa Palazzo; and to our knowledgeable project supervisor, Joy Aquilino, for making the entire process go so smoothly.

A very special thank you to Milton Cooper for his technical expertise and for his help with graphic layout and design through the entire creation of this book. He even managed to get us and our projects to the photo studio! We also thank him for handcrafting the stool and for executing the design and handcrafting the table on page 7. His support has been invaluable.

Additionally, Gail thanks: Stephen Cooper, my son, who, without my realizing it, has quite successfully grown up and given me such wise advice and encouragement; Richard Salomon, my brother, for taking care of me—yet again—and his wife Susan; and my other siblings, Linda, Burt, and Warren, who are always with me.

Dee thanks: my children, Laurie Gilkes and Peter Davis, for their constant support and encouragement; my grandchildren, Amy Gilkes and Conner Davis, who shared so many happy hours with me, cutting and pasting in my studio; my good friend, Alice Straus, who has shopped the world for prints and papers for my collection.

COVER: The exotic box illustrates a harmonious combination of subject and object, with scintillating colors and Eastern images (found on page 45). We cut the print on page 77 to fit the inner hexagonal area of the plate, and then painted the border in a metallic rust color. On the heart-shaped box, Redouté's large *Gloxinie* image (page 35) was a bold choice for such a small surface.

PAGE 2: The unusual oriental scrap complements the shape of this black wood box. The roof (lid) lifts up to reveal a painted metallic celadon interior. Wearable art is one of today's fashions. You can cover a bracelet with gold Chinese "good luck" paper (page 47), paint the inside black, and add some Chinese calligraphy. Try some scrap on an armful of bracelets.

ABOVE: We recycled Stephen Cooper's old chair for Dee's grandson, Conner Davis, painting it in primary colors and using the theater and circus themes on page 109. Notice the circus-ring composition on the chair seat. The picture frame continues the playful circus theme.

Senior Editor: Joy Aquilino
Project Editor: Alisa Palazzo
Designer: Areta Buk
Production Manager: Hector Campbell

First published in 2001 by Watson-Guptill Publications, a division of BPI Communications, Inc., 770 Broadway, New York, NY 10003
www.watsonguptill.com

Copyright © 2001 Dee Davis and Gail B. Cooper

Library of Congress Cataloging-in-Publication Data
Davis, Dee.
    The decoupage gallery : a collection of over 450 color and 550 black-and-white design motifs / Dee Davis and Gail B. Cooper.
        p. cm.
    ISBN 0-8230-1289-1
    1. Decoupage.   I. Cooper, Gail B.   II. Title.
TT870 .D2955 2001
745.54'6—dc21

00-042873

Manufactured in Malaysia

2 3 4 5 6 7 8 / 07 06 05 04 03 02 01

CONTENTS

INTRODUCTION

Decorating with paper is by no means a new art form. From school children to professional artists, people in every country have engaged in the folk art of papercutting with either scissors or knives. In fact, paper has been used for decorative and artistic purposes throughout the world ever since the Chinese originated papermaking over 2,000 years ago.

With the invention of the printing press in the 15th century, publishers were able to reproduce an innumerable variety of images. By the 16th century, inexpensive engravings and etchings by famous artists were available in every conceivable subject and style. Imitating sought-after Oriental lacquerware, the late 17th-century Venetians were the first to expertly decorate their furniture with chinoiserie engravings that were handcolored, cut out, glued down on a surface, and then protected with varnish. This technique became extremely popular and flourished throughout 18th-century Europe, where people embellished every available surface, from walls and large screens to furniture and fans.

In France, Marie Antoinette and the ladies at court spent hours cutting up original engravings by François Boucher, Jean-Honoré Fragonard, Jean Baptiste Pillement, and Antoine Watteau. It is the French name for this technique, *decoupage* (from the verb *decouper,* to cut out), that has prevailed, although different countries had other names for this scissors art. In England, for example, it was called Japanning, referring to the popular lacquer furniture from the Far East. One of several Italian names was *arte povero* (poor man's art) because of the use of engravings, which were less expensive than actual paintings.

Many manuals of ornamental designs and pictures were published in Germany, England, Italy, and Japan in the 18th century. These picture book albums contained an encyclopedic variety of subjects and themes. Technical developments in color lithography during the 19th century allowed for consistent quality and less expensive pictures. So, at a time when travel to far away places was limited, almost anyone could afford the illustrated books, posters, maps, and drawings of plants and animals that brought the outside world home. It's no wonder that so many people collected these prints.

In 19th-century England, collecting Victorian "scrap" pictures became the rage. These mass-produced sheets of colored images were die cut, often embossed, and covered a variety of subject matter, much of it extremely sentimental. A favorite pastime for people of all ages was creating scrap albums, which is now so very popular again! Whole families entertained themselves at home covering everything available with scrap. Queen Victoria was an avid collector and the Duke of Wellington himself covered several screens with a mix of scrap and engravings.

Major artists of the 20th century created two-dimensional mixed media, combining paper with paint on their canvases. The avant-garde collages of Georges Braque and Pablo Picasso included newsprint, wrappers, ticket stubs, and patterned and textured papers, that were both cut and torn. There was further experimentation with assemblage, a medium of three-dimensional construction that used "found" objects, papers, fabrics, and almost anything in a surreal stretch of the imagination. The artist Joseph Cornell placed his assemblages inside "found" old, wood boxes—called box art—frequently covering the front with glass. Henri Matisse's superb scissors sculpted shapes from paper, a process he described as "drawing with scissors." The shapes and colors in his cut-paper collages have been endlessly appropriated and recycled in every possible medium.

Existing prints and engravings from the 18th and 19th centuries are too valuable and much too fragile to even think of using for cutting and pasting. Instead, use the reproductions in this book, carefully selected from our treasured collection, which you can cut and paste without causing problems. As you'll see from the photographs, you can use these motifs in many ways: alone or in combination with the backgrounds and borders, both colored or in black and white. It's fascinating to explore and experiment with all the different techniques. Let your imagination flow! Your flights of fancy are your opportunities to express yourself, your personality, and your taste.

We wish you all the joy that comes with the process of creating: from choosing the object and the prints, to painting, cutting, composing, and gluing to the final sanding, varnishing, and polishing when magically it all comes together . . . your own work of art!

The 18th-century Print Room Style traditionally used whole prints, framed in borders and hung from bows, to decorate walls. We adapted this style for this table, using the antique engravings on pages 25, 27, and 29; the bows on page 170; and the borders on page 172. The stool, painted in pale pastel colors, displays pictures from our antique scrap collection. You can even cover an antique wood shoe form with scrap.

A background of handwriting lines the inside of the waste basket, on top of which we scattered a few flowers cut from a larger flower picture. The same floral print is on the handmarbled wood plate, the white flowers predominating. For the frame, we found inspiration for the color combination of pink and yellow in Monet's garden at Giverny. (Prints on waste basket and plate: page 33; for the frame: page 43.)

DECOUPAGE BASICS

When you invest a lot of time and energy in your creation, you want to ensure that it will endure for years to come. Quality products, though usually more expensive, have greater durability. It is worthwhile to buy the best for the best results. Then simply follow the clear instructions to ensure that your work will flow smoothly to completion. Don't be afraid; the more you do, the better you do it. There are no fatalities here; mistakes can be corrected, there are ways to camouflage and repair. Relax and enjoy yourself with this comforting quotation from John Ruskin:

> *All things are literally better, lovelier and more beloved for the imperfections that reflect the human effort that went into their making.*

Have a wonderful time!

WORKING WITH PRINTS

Whether you're designing albums, making assemblages and collages, or decorating with decoupage, you'll need a large variety of printed papers. The means to express yourself successfully requires printed images in a wide range of subject matter and styles.

COLLECTING

Now is the time to get out those bits and pieces of memorabilia that you've saved: programs, invitations, tickets, labels, stamps, photographs, and so on. The memorabilia you've saved for years can be used together with the motifs, borders, and other images in this book. Once you start accumulating a number of papers, it's helpful to organize and sort them by subject. Place them in plastic bags and store them flat, in labeled boxes. This will keep your collection clean, unwrinkled, and away from the light to protect from fading.

A medium-weight paper with a smooth, matte finish will work the best. Paper that is too thin will wrinkle when you apply glue to it, and the background color of the surface could show through. Paper that is too thick will be harder to manage during delicate cutting, and covering it will require extra coats of finish. In addition, printing inks can bleed, sink into porous paper, and fade. For example, beautiful wrapping paper is not made to last; it fades and becomes brittle as harmful acids destroy the fibers.

With experience, you'll be able to feel the differences in paper weights and textures, and know which will work best for you. If you are deeply concerned with preservation, research all the products you plan to use. Make sure that anything you purchase is labeled "archival quality" and is acid-free and non-toxic.

SELECTING

Your choice of prints is your means of self-expression and should reflect your own taste and individuality. However, we offer some guidelines to help with your decisions. When choosing images for a project, either from this book to coordinate with your collectibles or from another source, select items that offer a variety of images and are harmonious in color, style, and scale.

This group of images usually determines the style of the object to be decoupaged. The scale of the selected images should be in proportion to the size and shape of the object to which they will be applied. Note that you'll need more prints than you might think; after you cut away all the

excess paper surrounding the prints, you'll have a lot less material. Keep in mind that a three-dimensional object normally has at least four sides and a top, and you may want to add a surprise on the inside or even on the bottom.

Whether you start with a whole picture, prefer intricate cutting, or use a combination of both these techniques, you'll find many choices that work well together. Cut, tear, color, combine, and compose together with the pictures, borders, and motifs. Your visual creation can be mainly decorative, or it can tell a story, celebrate an occasion, relate to a theme, create an heirloom, or make a personal statement. Then expand on that choice, and enhance it with as many variations and details as you wish in your own taste and style.

Take snapshots, newsprint, engraved announcements, matchbook covers, and other collected papers to the copy shop. Working with copies is easier and safer than using your originals. With the new laser copiers you can change both size and color, reverse images, and produce them in multiples. You might want to keep this book for your reference library and photocopy the images, adjusting them to suit your needs. To use the black-and-white images starting on page 129, which are printed on both sides of each page, you can either photocopy them or apply a coat of opaque white paint to the images on the back of a page and let this dry before cutting out the images on the front.

PREPARING PRINTS: BASIC STEPS

1. Add color, if desired; draw ladders, which will be removed just prior to gluing (see page 18).
2. Seal front of print; if prints are to be placed under glass, seal back.
3. Cut out prints, including borders.

COLORING

Prints that are already colored seldom need changing, but you can make adjustments if you like. You can use a non-abrasive vinyl eraser to lighten an area that's too dark. With colored artist's oil pencils, you can add a touch more color, thicken very thin lines, and color white paper edges or even fill in tiny background areas instead of cutting them away.

This is the time to pencil in "ladders" to temporarily support fine details and delicate images that are attached in only one place to the main part of a form (the antennae of a butterfly or the leaf of a flower, for example). As you cut out the image, also cut around these ladders, leaving them on to provide the added stability. Keep the ladders on until just before gluing, when you should cut them off. (See pages 12 and 18.)

Handcoloring black-and-white prints can involve adding anything from a simple color wash to a varied, detailed palette. You want permanent, transparent—never opaque—color, whether you use artist's oil pencils, acrylic paints, or colored inks. Choose your favorite colors and practice on extra photocopies or papers. Beginners should start with a simple palette, just two or three colors, and even a monochromatic color scheme can be very effective. A non-abrasive vinyl eraser will remove artist's pencils, so mistakes are fixable. When finished, spray sealing is a must!

As an alternative or in addition to coloring, before sealing and cutting, you can easily antique black-and-white prints by tinting with one or two washes of cold, black coffee or tea. Sponge it over the print, blot off any puddles, let dry, then seal. With soy sauce, we turned a background paper just the right shade of taupe!

Permanent markers are handy for coloring borders and decorative ornamental effects, and also for adding your signature.

SEALING

After coloring your prints, but prior to cutting them, you should seal them with one coat of a liquid, brush-on, water-soluble acrylic sealer that dries quickly. This is as a multi-purpose sealer that can be used for paper, wood, or other surfaces. (It also comes in a heavier weight that is mainly for wood.) Sealing is very important as it strengthens the paper and protects the colors from running during gluing. Using a poly brush (see page 14), seal the front of the print, and let it dry before cutting it out. For pieces that you intend to place under glass, do the reverse: Seal the back of the print, rather than the front. For very large prints or large paper backgrounds, you should seal both the front and back of the paper to prevent wrinkling.

We handcolored and reversed the cherub (found on page 140) for the plate, adding a bow and some flowers. Two layers of sheer white rice paper create the translucent alabasterlike background. The letter holder has cupids (pages 141 and 142) both inside and outside. The little valentine box makes a sentimental gift for a special person (page 115). And, dare we mention dog tags to cat lovers? To make an ID tag, try a picture of a child or even a pet, and print the subject's name on the back with marker.

CUTTING

Decoupage is a "scissors art." Careful cutting of details, reshaping a flower or leaf, as well as special highlighting of certain elements (feathers on a bird, for example) are most important to the final look of your project. You'll need curved scissors to cut curved shapes and straight scissors to cut straight lines. Almost all your cutting will require a pair of curved, small, sharp manicure scissors, as only small blades can cut fine, intricate details. Solingen steel is the best quality and stays sharp the longest. Surgical scissors, curved with narrow blades, are fine, too. A craft or X-Acto knife or scalpel is also useful, because its narrow, pointed, sharp edge easily cuts small interior spaces in prints. In addition, paper-edger scissors cut deckle, scallop, serrated, and many other special-effect edges.

Mastering skillful detailed cutting requires practice using the curved manicure scissors. Practice with magazine pictures, changing and improving the shapes as you go. When you feel some confidence with these new skills, you are ready to tackle your prints.

If you are right-handed, hold the scissors in your right hand with your thumb and third finger. The scissors will rest on, and be supported by, the index finger. Hold the paper loosely in your left hand, and feed it to the scissors, turning it around and back as you cut. Point the scissors to the right, with the points curving away from the paper, providing a clear view of the cutting edge. (See below). The right hand just opens and closes the scissors, which remain in the same position, while the left hand moves the paper. If you are left-handed, reverse the holding instructions and practice until you're comfortable. Most importantly, relax! Don't clutch the scissors tightly; a sharp blade will cut with gentle pressure. You do, however, need bright light to see your work, and nice

soothing music helps, too. Above all, never panic. There are always more images for you to use, and anything cut off by mistake can always be glued back together.

To begin, cut away excess paper surrounding the selected image. When possible, cut the print into smaller, easier-to-hold sections. Before cutting the outer edges of a print, first cut around all the interior details. This gives you more paper to hold onto while you're cutting and prevents outside cut edges from breaking off. Do this by poking a small hole in areas of unprinted paper interior. Then, holding the scissors underneath the paper, bring the tips of the scissors up through the hole and begin to cut the background away. A sharp pointed craft knife is helpful in cutting interior areas, too. After cutting out several images, turn them over to see if the silhouette of the shape identifies the subject or if further cutting is needed to refine any of the shapes. Then spread the images face up on a piece of black paper to make sure there are no telltale white edges showing; if there are, either cut away the white or color it to match the print.

In addition to basic cutting, there are also a number of interesting techniques you can use to enhance prints, photographs, and other papers. Serrated cutting—wiggling the paper back and forth as you cut it—creates texture. You can improve the shape of a picture by cutting it into a circle, oval, or octagon using a template. Cut fancy edges with special paper-edger scissors, or deckle the edges by carefully tearing the surrounding paper away. Frame the whole picture with a decorative border. Other options are to outline cut edges with paint, colored pencil, or permanent ink or marker, in a color that coordinates with the colors of the print, or to just outline them in gold or silver. (See pages 10–11 for more information on coloring your prints.)

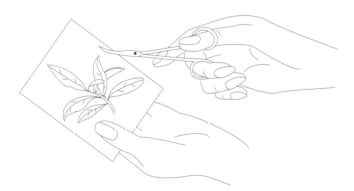

ABOVE: If you are right-handed, hold the paper in your left hand and the scissors in your right; do the reverse if you are left-handed.

RIGHT: The Xs indicate areas that should now be cut away. The dotted lines indicate the penciled-in ladders, which you should cut around just as if they were part of the image. But, don't forget to cut them off just before you glue down your image.

SUCCESSFUL CUTTING STRATEGIES

First cut away excess background paper. Then cut down the size of the less important elements and create details from shapes that aren't clearly defined, such as the green, leaf areas and the edges of the branches here.

When cutting out whole images, such as these amusing medieval men, use parts of the whole from a duplicate print to accompany the full images.

Cutting away most of the background sharpens the focus, as with these horses. Notice the reverse cutting (cutting into the image) across the bottom, eliminating the straight line and creating an interesting silhouette.

PREPARING YOUR SURFACE

Start with fairly easy projects before you tackle that grand piano or long wall. Look around the room you're in; surely there's something there that doesn't please your eye, some needy object that calls for enhancement. Choose from the wide variety of unadorned surfaces waiting for you: old, new, wood, metal, glass, plastic, marble, papier-mâché, ceramics, almost any rigid surface will do.

Search the attic, basement, and back of the closet; go to tag sales and thrift shops. Look in arts and crafts shops, home improvement centers, and houseware stores, or try mail order catalogs until you find that box, plate, or wastebasket that's just what you want. Consider "found objects": a rock, piece of driftwood, seashell, or old clay pot, for example. When you travel, treasure hunting for different objects to decoupage makes any trip more fun.

We recommend that you start on a small (but not miniature) object with a simple shape and flat surface, such as a plaque, flat frame, or small tray. While you're learning on this, you can think about all the other things you want to decoupage: lamps, screens, tables, footstools, planters, vases. As long as you prepare an object's surface, you can magically transform "junk" into a conversation piece or family heirloom, both beautiful and useful.

SURFACE PREPARATION: BASIC STEPS

FOR WOOD AND METAL:

1. Repair as needed, and (for wood) sand until smooth; then remove residue and wipe clean with a tack cloth.
2. To paint the surface: seal it first, apply two to three coats of paint (lightly sanding smooth before final coat of paint), clean thoroughly with a tack cloth, and seal again.
3. To stain a wood surface: clean with a tack cloth, stain, and seal.

FOR GLASS:

1. Wash clean, and dry with a lint-free chamois cloth.

SUPPLIES

We recommend using only brush-on, non-toxic, water-based materials, which are environmentally friendly and also safer for your health. Before you use a product, always read all labels and instructions, and follow them carefully. Be aware that environmental factors—such as humidity, extreme temperature changes, and both natural and artificial light—can not only affect paper and wood but can also affect the drying times of paints and finishes. When in doubt, test a product on a sample board prior to using it in a project. And just in case, have the solvent for any material you're using close at hand.

CHAMOIS CLOTH (NATURAL). A lint-free cloth used to clean and dry glass.

MATTE MEDIUM OR MOD PODGE (MATTE). Applied to glass prior to paint application, these liquids allow for a better bond between paint and a glass or plastic surface. (Also see pages 18–19 for additional uses.)

PAINT. Acrylic or latex (water-based) paint comes in small jars and wonderful colors and gives smooth coverage when applied to clean surfaces with paint roller or poly brush. Don't use tube acrylics (they'll show brushstrokes) or glossy enamel paint (it repels glue and finish). Occasionally turn stored jars upside down to re-disperse the pigment.

PAINT ROLLER. Use a short-nap paint roller for applying the final coats of a paint or finish, since it leaves no texture or brushstrokes. Buy a size appropriate for the size of your surface.

POLY BRUSH. An inexpensive foam sponge on a handle used to apply coats of paint, sealer, and finish smoothly. Buy the 1-inch size for smaller surfaces and the 2-inch size for larger areas. Be sure to dampen the brush *slightly* before using. Wash in warm soapy water to clean.

SANDING BLOCK. A small, felt-padded wood block to use for dry sanding. This keeps the surface level. To use, wrap the sandpaper around the block, and secure it around the top with a rubber band. A small felt blackboard eraser does nicely as a makeshift sanding block.

SANDING SPONGE. The fine or extra fine grade (manufactured by 3M) safely and easily sands paint smooth.

SANDPAPER. Used for smoothing and polishing, sandpaper is graded from coarse grit (80 and up) to extra fine (500 and up). The lower the number, the coarser the grit. Remove old paint, stain, varnish, or rust with a very coarse grit paper. Sand raw wood with a medium grit (garnet/tan) paper, about 240. To use, cut larger sheets into quarters; it's easier to handle.

SEALER. Use liquid acrylic water-soluble brush-on sealer to protect your project from damage. It is quick-drying and comes as a multi-purpose sealer for paper, wood, and other surfaces, or in a heavier weight that is mainly for wood. Prime metal, bisque, wood, and other materials with wood or metal sealers or primers. Seal porous surfaces before painting to prevent paint from sinking into the surface and wood resin from bleeding through the paint. Seal painted surfaces before gluing down any decoupage images to protect the paint from damage. On wood surfaces that are only to be stained, sealer is applied after staining. On wood surfaces that are to be painted, sealer is applied both prior to and after paint application. (See box on page 14.) When in doubt, seal. Be on the safe side.

SMALL SPONGES OR FOAM SQUARES. For patting paint onto glass.

SPRAY PAINTS, SEALERS, AND FINISHES. Preferably non-toxic, for use on baskets and intricately carved wood details for which application with a brush really won't work.

STAIN. For use on wood surfaces, wood stain is a transparent color wash that is applied to unsealed wood and highlights its grain.

STEEL WOOL. Use a coarse grade to remove rust from metal and fine to smooth stained and painted surfaces. The very fine #0000 is used for the final polishing.

TACK CLOTH. Sticky cheesecloth to remove dust/residue. Store in sealed plastic bag to prevent it from drying out.

WOODWORKER'S GLUE. This is specifically recommended for maximum-strength bonding together of wood.

CLEANING, SANDING, AND SEALING

Your goal when preparing any item for decoupage is to achieve a clean, dry, smooth, even surface. A good, inexpensive idea for protecting your work area and simplifying clean-up is to cut a plastic drop cloth into sections, layer the sections one on top of the other on your work table, and discard the top piece when it's dirty. When preparing a surface, always keep your tack cloth handy, and use it every step of the way—after sanding and before the application of every coat of sealer, paint, and finish—to keep the surface dust free. Denatured alcohol will remove grease and stubborn dirt on old surfaces if soap and water don't do it.

FOR WOOD: Repair any cracks and cover any knotholes with wood filler or spackling paste. Let dry before sanding.

Natural wood is currently very popular. We sealed these wood place mats and then cut out and glued the colorful fruit (on pages 51 and 53) along the outside curves. The candleshade of brown wrapping paper is perfectly suited to the subject: monkeys cavorting among hand-colored palm fronds (page 49). Happily, we also had one monkey left for a coaster, backed with handmade paper.

Sand the surface, going with the grain and progressing from coarse to fine sandpaper. Wipe off any residue with a tack cloth. Seal well with sealer, or coat with a primer before painting.

FOR METAL OR TINWARE: Remove any rust with coarse, dry steel wool. Wash the surface with detergent, and rinse and dry thoroughly. Seal well with sealer, or prepare with a metal primer.

FOR GLASS: Wash in soapy water, and rinse with diluted ammonia or white vinegar. Rinse again, and dry with a lint-free chamois cloth.

OTHER POROUS SURFACES: Bisque (fired, unglazed ceramics) and other porous items need to be well sealed with the appropriate sealer.

CHOOSING A SURFACE COLOR

There are many things to consider when choosing a color for your surface, keeping in mind that this color should enhance your prints. For a harmonious background, you can select a hue that is an accent color in your prints. For a traditional piece, follow the colors of that style or period. In addition, dark colors are dramatic, especially in a greater intensity than the dominant print color. (See bookends on opposite page.) An assortment of colored tissue or construction paper, spread out around your prints, will guide your eye to the best selection.

Whatever your choice, have fun with color; add details, try a stripe or band of contrasting color, lightly texture a background by sponging a lighter or darker shade over the base paint application, or paint the lid or inside of a box another color. Remember: You can always paint over anything if you don't like what you've done.

APPLYING COLOR

Attaining good, even coverage is not always easy. Practice first on some sample boards before working on your actual surface. With patience and practice, you will achieve a smooth, rich coating of paint. The following application techniques apply to any allover coating material, whether it's paint, sealer, or finish.

FOR OPAQUE COLOR: Coats that are too thin will take forever to cover a surface, and coats that are too thick will take forever to dry and will usually crack. A medium coat is just right. Dampen a poly brush in water, and dip it halfway into the paint. Holding the brush at a 45-degree angle, not upright, apply the paint to your surface using light pressure (otherwise you'll cause bubbles). Always apply the paint in the same direction (with the grain on wood), and start each stroke of a loaded brush at the center of an unpainted area of the surface, working back into an already-coated area.

Whenever possible, it's best to apply the paint (or sealer or finish) to a flat, horizontal surface, turning the object as you coat it. With a box, do the sides first, then the top (rotating the box as you go so that the side you're working on is on top). This helps avoid paint drips; if you get drips and runs, use less paint on the brush. Brush with slightly overlapping, parallel strokes.

You should get good paint coverage applying three coats like this. Don't rush the drying time for each coat. Lightly sand with fine (320) sandpaper or a sanding sponge before the final coat. If you have trouble getting even coverage, use a paint roller for the last coat. Let the surface dry thoroughly before sealing (six hours is fine).

FOR TRANSPARENT COLOR: Use a stain or transparent color wash, and apply with a poly brush or cloth in the direction of the grain to unsealed wood. Let this dry, then seal it with the appropriate sealer.

ON GLASS OR PLASTIC: Pat on thin coats of paint with a piece of foam square or small sponge to avoid brush-strokes. On glass, pat on a thin coat of matte medium or Mod Podge with a small foam sponge before applying any paint to get a better bond.

The flowers (from page 39) on the frame for this invitation matched the color scheme of the wedding. We also placed some on the right-most coaster. The red marble border, cut from page 127, frames the invitation and bands the pencil cup (holding flowers here). We used miniature French flower bouquets (page 31) on the pencil cup and other two coasters, cut out and backed with pale peach tissue paper on one, used whole and backed with green rice paper on the other.

COMPOSITION

Once you've prepared your surface, you're ready to decide the placement of the images to appear on it. One of the main tools you'll need for this is plastic adhesive (Hold It)—a removable, reusable white putty used to temporarily place and replace cutouts in position while you compose. Drafting tape, or a removable transparent tape, also works. Long, bent-nosed tweezers enable you to pick up, move, and place small cutouts easily.

To begin, spread your cutouts, borders, and papers around your object. Try every possibility, using temporary adhesive to hold the cutouts in place. Place any borders and then the largest cutouts, before filling in spaces with smaller pieces. Don't overlap pieces unless working with very thin papers or putting a composition under glass. Multiple layers of paper create uneven surfaces. It's preferable to fit pieces together like a jigsaw puzzle.

Your goal is an eye-catching, pleasing design. Variations in print sizes, shapes, and colors create a rhythmic flow of design and color. Symmetry can be static, so try groups of uneven numbers of elements with unequal spaces between them. Off-center placements can be more dramatic than centered ones. Create curves, rather than straight lines, with your images. Move a continuous design around an edge—but don't bend a person or animal. It's surreal. Do bend a flower, leaf, or branch. As you work, check your composition carefully from a distance. Squint so that details diminish and you see more easily if spacing can be improved. Set the object on a lazy Susan and slowly turn it all the way around. Check your work at the level it will be seen. For example, take a wastebasket off the table and look at it on the floor.

Sometimes arrangement problems become obvious if you turn a temporarily composed piece upside down; then you just focus on the positive shapes and the spaces between them. Look at some lace to see how important those open, negative spaces are. Create interesting, varied negative spaces as you compose. Move a cutout around the composition to see how relationships change. Once you're pleased with your composition, stop designing and move on to gluing. (See page 18.)

The outside of an object is not always the only surface to decorate. It's a nice surprise to add a cutout, border, or paper lining inside a box. A personal message, including your signature and the date, is also nice. First practice any writing on scrap paper. Use a fine-tipped permanent marker, which is easier to use than a very small brush.

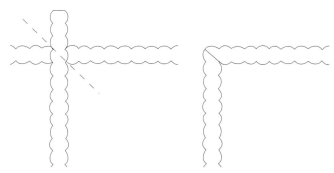

If using a border, put it in place before arranging the cutouts. If you're creating a frame, miter the corners by cutting through the two overlapping pieces of border on the diagonal, before gluing them down.

Composition (as well as color) can create many optical illusions. Observe the Reversible Vase *by Edgar Rubin. See a vase? Look again and there's a pair of silhouetted profiles!*

These are some examples of simple composition and cutting. Visualize these objects without the borders, marble banding, or dramatic dark backgrounds, and you'll realize the importance of these elements. Also, the red interior is a nice surprise when you open the little box decoupaged with 18th-century animal prints (page 165). (Bookend images: pages 56–57; tray and cup images: page 151).

GLUING

When you are satisfied with your composition, you are ready to glue all the cutouts in place on your surface. This is an exciting moment. Don't rush, work slowly and carefully. Mistakes can be corrected.

> ## GLUE APPLICATION
> Apply glue to the back of a print, and press the print in the outline on your surface. Roll over it with a brayer, and clean off any excess glue around it. When the glue is dry, burnish the edges of the print.
>
> ### WHEN GLUING UNDER GLASS:
> Apply matte medium to the back of the glass, and press the print in the outline, front side facing the glass. Clean off any excess glue around the print.

SUPPLIES

BRAYER. A rubber roller with a handle, used to flatten out prints after gluing by pressing out air bubbles and excess glue. A 4-inch size can be used for almost everything. A round bottle or glass can substitute.

BURNISHER. This paddle-edged tool flattens out and embeds the edges of paper cutouts after the glue dries, leveling the surface. You can also substitute an orange wood manicure stick or demitasse spoon for this.

CHAMOIS CLOTH (NATURAL). A lint-free cloth to clean and dry glass or mirrors.

CHINA MARKER (GREASE PENCIL). To mark positioning outlines around cutouts on glass, prior to gluing. Marks are removable. An eyebrow pencil works for this, too.

CLOTH. An all-purpose, reusable, disposable cloth (such as Handi Wipes). Place it, slightly dampened, over cutouts before rolling with the brayer to absorb excess glue.

COLORED CHALK. To mark outlines around cutouts prior to gluing, indicating placement. The soft, dusty (dust-free is too hard) chalk won't indent the object's surface and it can be sharpened to a narrow point.

COTTON SWABS. For removing any excess glue.

CRAFT KNIFE. Handy for removing or repositioning a cutout that you've already glued down.

GLUE OR POLY BRUSH. For applying glue.

MATTE MEDIUM. Use this or matte Mod Podge to bond paper to glass or plastic; goes on milky but dries clear. Best for use on thinner papers, like tissue or rice paper.

SILICONE SEALANT. Packaged in tubes, it's not water-soluble but will keep hard-to-secure objects in place. Used mainly for assemblages (box art) and 3-D decoupage.

SPONGE. To press down cutouts when gluing.

TOOTHPICKS. Helpful for putting glue under small edges (of cutouts) that may have lifted.

WALLPAPER PASTE (CLEAR, READYMADE). An alternative to other adhesives because it dries slower, giving you more working time.

WATER. Keep a dish of water near your work area for cleaning up.

WAX PAPER OR PLASTIC WRAP. A good non-stick surface.

WHITE GLUE. An all-purpose glue (PVA—Elmer's or Sobo) for bonding paper to most surfaces except plastic. For heavier papers and trims use a heavier, tacky white glue.

BASIC GLUING PROCEDURE

Remember that you must have already sealed all your prints before you glue them down. (See page 11.) While your composition is still temporarily tacked down to your surface, draw an outline around the edges of the cutouts on the surface with chalk. Unless you're working with very thin papers or intend your composition to go under glass, papers should not overlap.

Starting with the largest pieces first, remove each cutout and glue on one piece at a time. Remove any tape or plastic adhesive and cut off any ladders. Place face down on wax paper. Being generous with the glue, apply an even coat of it over the entire back of a cutout and place it in the corresponding chalk outline. When you are working with delicate, lacy shapes, apply the glue to the object's surface, rather than to the cutout. Press the cutout gently into position with a slightly damp sponge or cloth, wiping away any excess glue at the edges. (Keep in mind that it's easier to clean off excess glue while it's still wet, rather than after it has completely dried.) Then lay a slightly moistened disposable cloth over the cutout and roll over it firmly with the brayer to press out air bubbles and extra glue. Clean again if necessary.

For very large prints or large paper backgrounds, seal both the front and back of the paper to prevent its wrinkling. Apply matte medium, Mod Podge, or wallpaper paste to the *object's surface* rather than to the print itself.

Once your papers are pasted down, allow four or five hours for the glue to dry. Clean off any residue of dried (shiny) glue around the prints with a cotton swab moistened in hot water. Check that all the pieces of paper are now completely attached to the surface, especially at their edges. If necessary, add more glue with a toothpick or small brush. Further flatten and embed the papers' sharp edges by pressing them gently with the burnisher.

GLUING UNDER GLASS

The gluing procedure is slightly different for work under glass. Mark the outlines of the cutouts on the *front* of the glass with a china marker. Start with the largest pieces. Remove and glue one piece at a time: Put a generous, thick coating of matte medium or Mod Podge on the *back* of the glass within the outline of the piece you are gluing. Press the *front* of the cutouts into the matte medium. With a slightly dampened cloth, press out any air bub-

bles, moving the bubbles toward the nearest edge. Don't press out too much matte medium, otherwise where there is not enough medium, there will be shiny areas on the print. Remove any residue at the edges of the cutouts, and clean the glass with a damp chamois cloth. The matte medium will dry clear in one or two hours.

After the glue is dry, you can apply the background. If you're applying a paper background to the glass, glue the paper to the glass and over the glued cutouts using matte medium or Mod Podge. If you're applying a painted background to the glass, first lightly pat a thin layer of matte medium or Mod Podge over the back of the glass and over the glued cutouts with a soft foam sponge, and let dry. This seals in the cutouts so that the paint won't get under their edges and ensures a better bond for the paint on the glass.

CHANGED YOUR MIND?

Remember that nothing is fatal; you can remove and reposition a cutout that you have glued down. Simply dip a cotton swab in very hot water, and dampen around an edge of the paper cutout. As the glue loosens, lift that edge with the tip of a small craft knife. Gradually work more hot water under the paper until it all lifts off. Let the paper dry before re-gluing.

This old, wood cigar box was a natural choice for these antique cigar box labels (from pages 65, 67, and 69). It took very little time to cut and finish but it has a great look. The scrapbook, with its vintage cars, stamps, and postcards (from pages 63 and 73), was a gift for a car buff who also loves to travel. The steamship flags hang from a piece of glued-down white string. The card box is decorated with 19th-century playing cards (from page 61) on a black pearl iridescent background.

FINISHING AND POLISHING

The complete finishing procedure is to apply multiple coats of finish, wet-sand the finished surface, polish it, and as a final step, wax it. Coating with finish serves two purposes, practical and aesthetic. Practically, these transparent finish layers protect your work from damage; aesthetically, they mellow and unify the whole piece, giving it depth and a lovely patina.

Most decorated surfaces require the permanent protection of finishing. The directions in this section—including the necessary number of coats of finish—apply to all rigid background surfaces, such as wood, metal, or plastic. On a nonrigid surface, such as chipwood or papier-mâché, apply only two or three coats. Framed artwork protected by glass does not need any finish applications. You might consider protecting a decorated album cover with a sheet of clear plastic contact. Boxed art, if not covered by glass, would benefit from a few coats of spray finish.

FINISHING

FINISH APPLICATION: BASIC PROCEDURE

Wipe the surface with a tack cloth before applying each coat of finish. Apply multiple coats, building up to 8 to 10 coats if you'll be wet-sanding, and 3 coats if you'll just be polishing. Allow the finish to dry thoroughly between coats.

We've found water-based acrylic polyurethane to be the best for a crystal-clear, durable finish. Finishes are usually available in gloss, satin, or matte sheens. Since gloss provides the hardest finish, start your finish application with that; then, if you wish, you can switch to matte sheen for the final coats. We recommend buying small cans of finish since, once opened, they don't have a long shelf life. Also, always have a dish of the appropriate solvent next to you when working; for water-based acrylic polyurethane, the solvent would be water. It's best to stay with acrylic varnish as oil-based varieties are toxic, and even the palest oil-based furniture varnish will yellow with age.

When doing a number of projects, you can work faster finishing several pieces at one time in production-line style. You'll need the following materials, and then proceed to the steps below:

CONTAINER. A small glass or plastic container with a cover to hold the finish you're working with during a project.

CRAFT STICK. For stirring finish.

FINISH. Water-based acrylic polyurethane is used to give decorated objects permanent protection. It's a milky liquid that quickly dries clear and hard. Again as with all materials, follow the instructions and recommendations on the label as to application and drying times.

JAR. A large container on which to prop objects for drying.

POLY BRUSH. For applying finish, but you can also use a paint roller when working on very large areas.

STRAIGHT PIN. Handy for popping air bubbles in the finish.

TACK CLOTH. Use before applying each coat of finish.

WATER. Always keep a dish of water or the appropriate solvent on hand while you are applying finish.

1. Clean the surface to be finished by going over it with the tack cloth. If any cutout edges lift off, re-glue them.
2. Dampen the poly brush.
3. Gently stir the finish in its can with a craft stick, then pour as much as you'll need for one coat into a clean container and close the finish can tightly.
4. Apply the finish following the same techniques given in the painting instructions for applying opaque color. (See page 16.) This type of finish quickly gets tacky, so don't overwork it. If you see an air bubble, pop it with the pin and don't worry; the next coat will fill this in.
5. Place your object (dry side down) on a tall jar or container to allow the air to circulate as the finish dries; then wash your brush in soapy water and rinse clean. Depending on the thickness of the application and the humidity in the air, it may take one to three hours to be dry enough to apply the next coat. Let each coat dry thoroughly. Moisture that hasn't completely evaporated will eventually cause cracking in the finish. Never force the drying process with a hair dryer, as this will cause problems later on: The object may be dry to the touch but not quite ready for the next coat. If the surface feels cold and clammy,

or your thumb leaves an imprint, wait! Some things cannot be hurried.

6. Apply a minimum of three coats of finish, adding more to surfaces that get heavier use; any surface that will be handled a lot needs more coats than one that will simply be a decorative piece. If you'll be wet-sanding, you may need to apply 8 to 10 coats of finish before you can sand without damaging the edges of the paper cutouts. If you're only applying two or three coats of finish, omit the wet sanding and move on to polishing.

WET SANDING

WET SANDING: BASIC PROCEDURE
Sand your object until it's smooth using soapy water and wet-dry sandpaper. Then, rinse off the soap and dry thoroughly.

Wet sanding will smooth the finish, eliminate brushstrokes and air bubbles, and best of all, magically diminish the surface differences and increase depth in appearance. Let your finished surface cure and harden for a day or two before wet-sanding. It's also a good idea to practice wet sanding first on a sample board or the bottom of your object. In general, wet sanding is usually started with a medium grit wet-dry (black) sandpaper. You can, if you wish, work up to the finer grits, such as 400 or 600. You'll need the following:

PAPER TOWELS. Choose soft absorbent ones for drying your piece.

SOAPY WATER. Fill a dish with warm, sudsy water. Use mild Ivory or Lux soap, not harsh detergent.

SPONGE. Choose a small flat sponge.

WET-DRY SANDPAPER. You'll need 320 or 400 grit.

1. Wrap a 1/4 sheet of wet-dry sandpaper around the flat sponge and saturate it with warm, soapy water.
2. Using medium pressure, sand the surface of your object, moving back and forth with the grain. Keep whichever side of the object you're working on horizontal to ensure an even surface. Keep the sponge well lubricated with suds. Wet-sand all the sides.

3. When the surface feels smooth as silk, rinse off the soap and dry the piece using a soft towel. The piece will now look very dull, but don't despair; move on to the polishing step to obtain a lovely sheen.

✣ OOPS! You've sanded through to the print or the paint? Stop at once and repair any damage using colored pencils and/or matching paint. Add several coats of finish before wet-sanding again.

POLISHING

POLISHING: BASIC PROCEDURE
Rub the surface with steel wool, then clean the residue with a tack cloth.

Polishing gives a soft sheen to your surface. As mentioned above, if you've applied only two or three coats of finish, omit the wet-sanding stage, and just follow the polishing instructions here. You will need:

STEEL WOOL. You'll need #0000 steel wool.

TACK CLOTH. Use this for lint-free wiping.

1. Polish your object with dry #0000 steel wool, rubbing back and forth with light pressure. This will smooth the surface and produce a soft sheen.
2. Wipe the surface with the tack cloth.

WAXING
After polishing your work, you have a few more options:
1. You can add a final perfect coat of gloss polyurethane finish to achieve a shiny surface, and then wax.
2. You can apply a coat of oil-based furniture varnish to get a mellow antique finish, and then wax. (Note: Here the solvent is turpentine.)
3. You can just wax the surface to achieve a matte finish.

Waxing is always the final step for protecting your work. Choose a colorless or white furniture wax and a few clean, soft cloths. Dampen one cloth, and apply a small amount of the furniture wax to it. Rub the wax over your object, wait a few minutes, and then buff with a dry cloth. This mellows the finish to a glowing patina only achieved with handrubbing. Like fine furniture, it occasionally needs to be re-waxed and buffed.

Have flowers all winter long by decorating objects, such as this candleshade
and candlestick, with floral images
(from pages 113 and 39 respectively).
It was great fun designing all four sides
of the tissue box to relate a romantic
story. To make Christmas ornaments,
buy undecorated wooden shapes or cut
your own from poster board or foam-
core board. Or, glue magnets on the
backs of the shapes to use on the fridge.
(We chose various pieces of our antique
scrap for these projects.)

THE PRINTS

Through the years, we've collected a large number of beautiful images. Now we happily share them here with you. Scanning through these pages will spark your imagination and vision, and inspire you with a wealth of ideas. You'll have a wonderful time choosing and using these rare and beautiful prints.

BASIC DECOUPAGE STEPS

Copy this outline and hang at your work table. If you need to refresh your memory as you're working, this is a handy reference.

PREPARING PRINTS

- Color, if desired; draw ladders.
- Seal front. (Under glass, seal back.)
- Cut out.

PREPARING SURFACES

- Repair as needed, sand, and clean with tack cloth.
- If painting: Seal, apply 2 to 3 coats of paint, sand, smooth, wipe with tack cloth, and seal again.
- If staining: Wipe with tack cloth, apply stain, seal.
- For glass: Wash glass, and dry with chamois cloth.

COMPOSING

- Place your cutouts, temporarily tacked down with plastic adhesive.
- Mark position of cutouts by outlining them with chalk. For cutouts under glass, mark position with china marker on *front* of glass.

GLUING

- Apply glue to back of print, press in place.
- Roll with brayer, clean, burnish edges when dry.
- For cutouts under glass: Apply matte medium to glass, press *front* of print in place. Clean. Pat on thin coat of matte medium if painting the background.

FINISHING

- Clean with tack cloth before applying each coat of finish.
- Build up multiple coats: 8 to 10 if wet-sanding, 3 coats if just polishing. Let surface dry thoroughly between coats.

WET SANDING

- Sand with a piece of wet-dry sandpaper and soapy water.
- Rinse off soap and dry thoroughly.

POLISHING

- Rub back and forth with #0000 steel wool.
- Wipe with tack cloth.

WAXING

- Buff with colorless furniture wax.

A Paris, Chez J. Marchand, Graveur, Rue St. Jacques, N° 3o.   *J. Baptiste Sculp.*

These rectangles can be reshaped
into circles or ovals. If cutting the
image away from the background,
do away with the wispy flowers.
See photo on page 16.

Tulipa Gesneriana!

Langlois.

Tulipe de Gesner.

Langlois. P.J. Redouté. — 141.

Gloxinia Var.

P.J. Redouté.— 137.

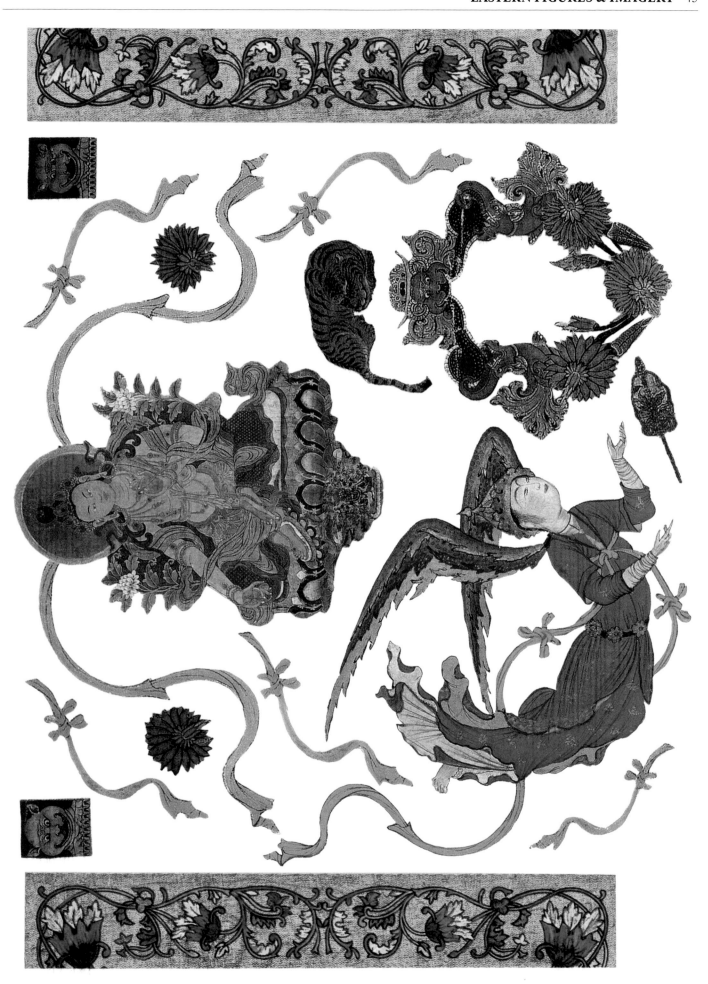

既使在石灣傳統藝術發展的高峰時期，藝術品的生產也是被限制的。葡萄牙律師文度士曾屢次出訪石灣，現歸澳門賈梅士博物館。玉書、陳渭岩、霍津和別堤及，石灣鎮產地。如果覺到藝術陶

精美的白瓷明清兩代由後，完全壓倒正是此時，它

廣東的藝術表現——石灣陶

施麗姬

從日常用品中發展出來

石灣陶瓷藝術的親切誘惑，可能歸於兩個原因產日用品的手工操作的普遍的藝術盛時，世界的注目御窯廠生產的瓷器上。

關於陽江陶。由於在陽江並沒有發現窯變釉的考古發掘資料，它的生產時期就很難以確定。不代的習慣稱法，藍白色的名(圖錄3-4)。月九到二十世紀，代的所謂"官"形式上與浙江器可能由浙江工匠的作品

確實如此，境地，正如成長為醞含廣人供奉食品以靈福尼亞洲的石灣陶藝已頻舊金山了。

據有關石灣歷史的傳聞，廣東省的陽江、東料或其他實物陶工的傳窯的後繼騷擾，背井離鄉，流的(圖錄1-10)

考古發掘砂和廉價盼者是和添陶土第陶始於一些可以的藝術價價值之外視，而不

既使在石生產也是文度士曾門賈梅士產地。如覺到藝術

精美的白明清兩代後，完全壓倒石灣、宜興和德化等類的地方窯。也正是此時，它們孕育出自己獨有的陶瓷藝師。

佛山的各種工藝相互刺激和影響，有些最突出的結晶陶工和戲曲的內在聯繫爾導致。石灣陶采戲曲，恐怕在他們面前演出，察工還從戲院的分類組祭行會他們生器、廟宇祭塑動物，屋頂瓦脊，這些構成了石灣陶的主要產品，特別是出口到東南亞的產品。行會規章限製它色為包大火黃、綠、藍，這也

期就藍白色的孔濁釉產品)。

的產品亦視為石灣窯白釉陶經營被定為代、明代或偶爾為漬飾以繩枝蓮凸花相似。這種月匠製成，它們與河工匠的作品形成鮮明對比。

陶工的作品形成鮮明對比。

也是他們的代表作。

津橋、建築裝飾傳統興戲曲愛好融合，結晶成為戲院寺廟屋頂上用長形陶歷史上破天荒的色彩圖錄 18-蘊強合成官府繁勝密集而生意繁宗生意。兩子屋頂(圖錄14-16)

變好融合，結晶成為長形陶的色彩錄 18-藝術陶的發

聞是否符實，石灣陶工燒製的多色品種的窯變勝於鈞釉，且不見於其他窯產品卻是事實。與官府

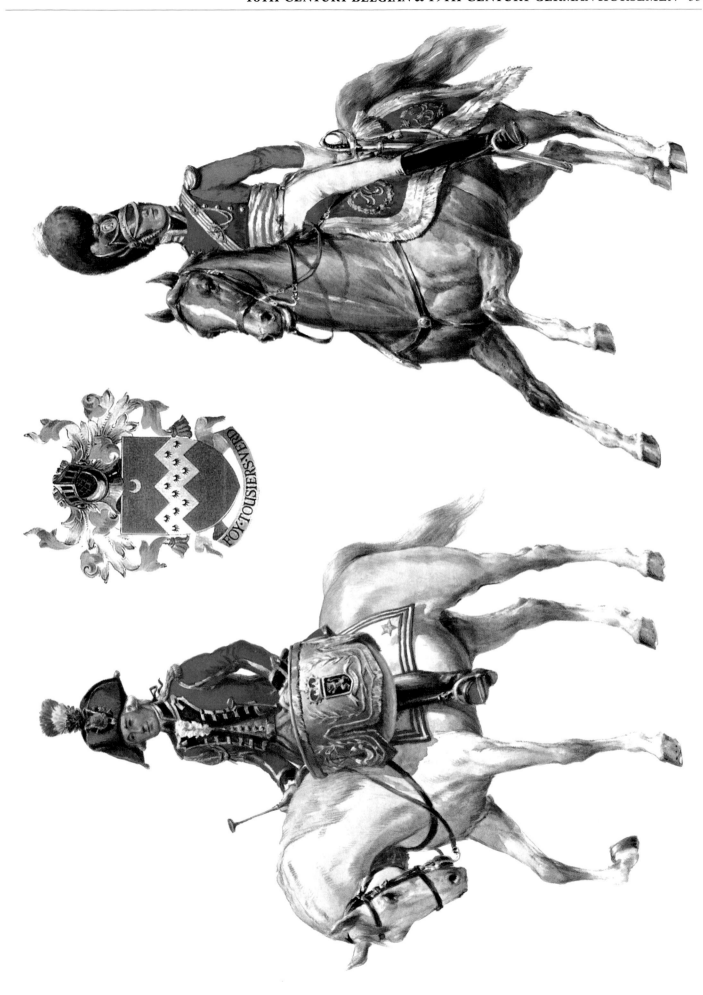

FOY·TOUSIERS·VERD

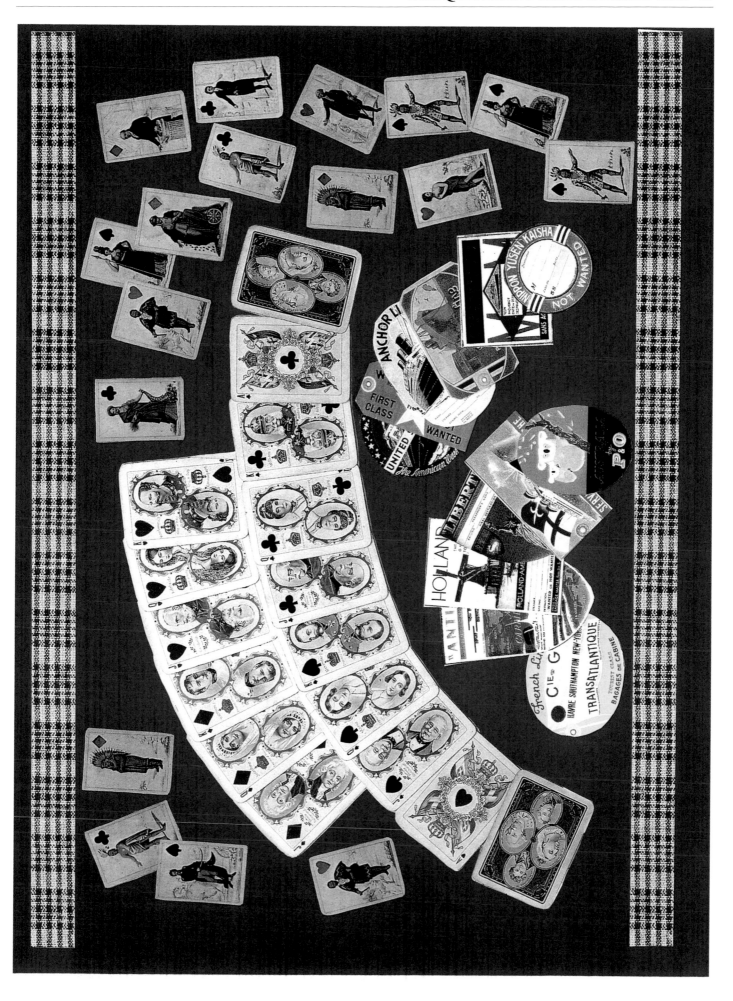

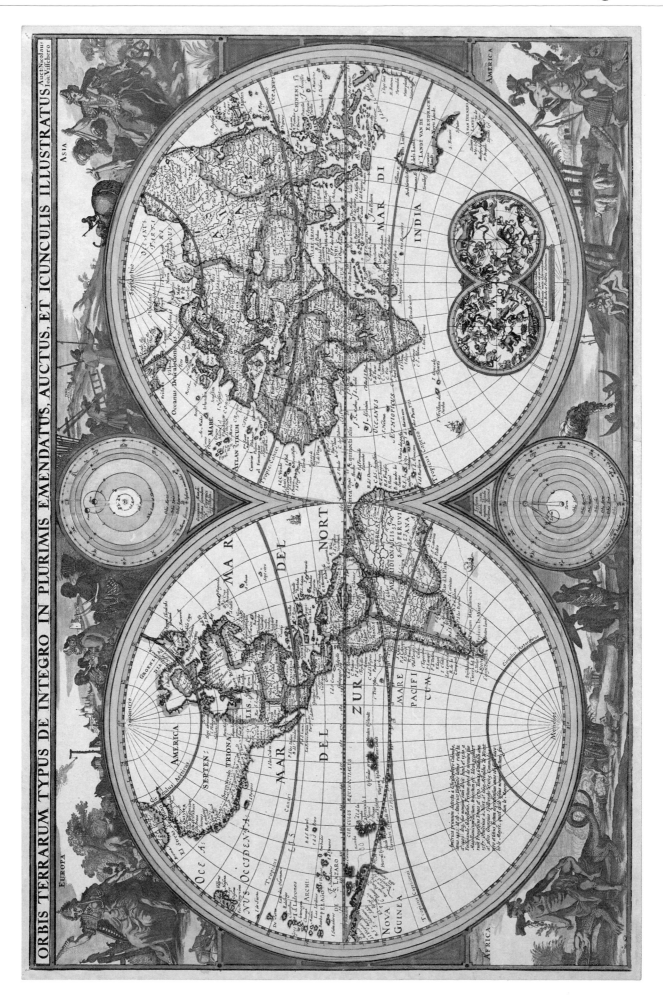

London Printed for Rob.t Sayer, Print & Map-Seller, opposite Fetter Lane, Fleet Street .

Alice B. Bunker.

A merry Christmas

LADIES'
COFFEE & LUNCH ROOM,
No. 23 Avon Street,
By T. D. COOK, Caterer.

Wishing you A Merry Christmas.

COMPLIMENTS OF THE SEASON.

REINDEER.

Love.

Jessie B. Bucker.

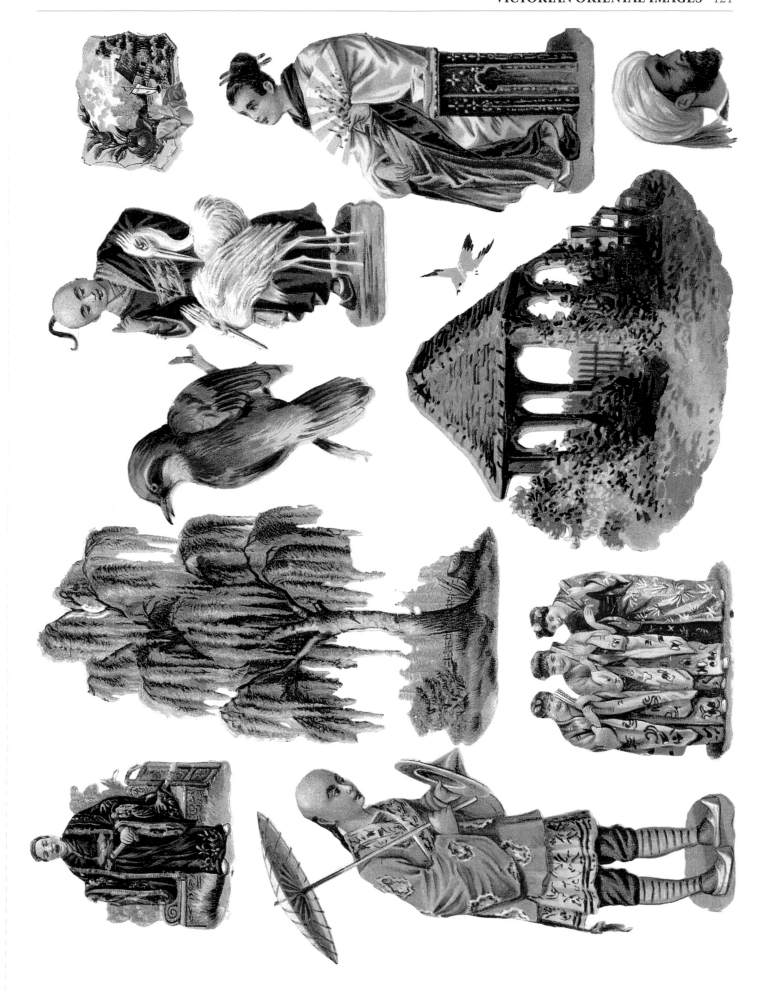

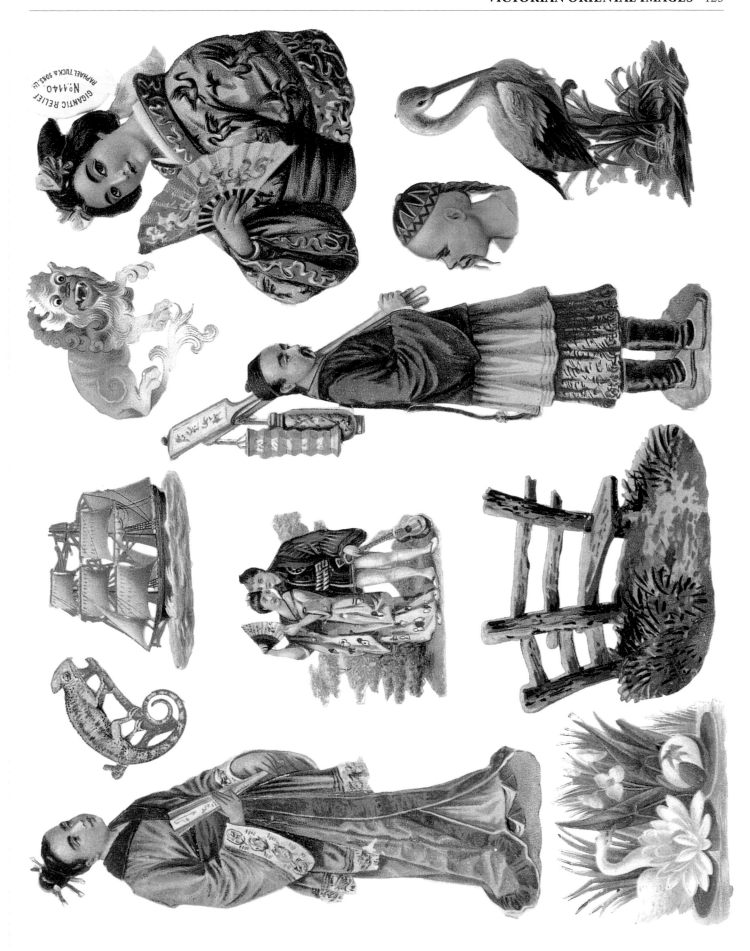

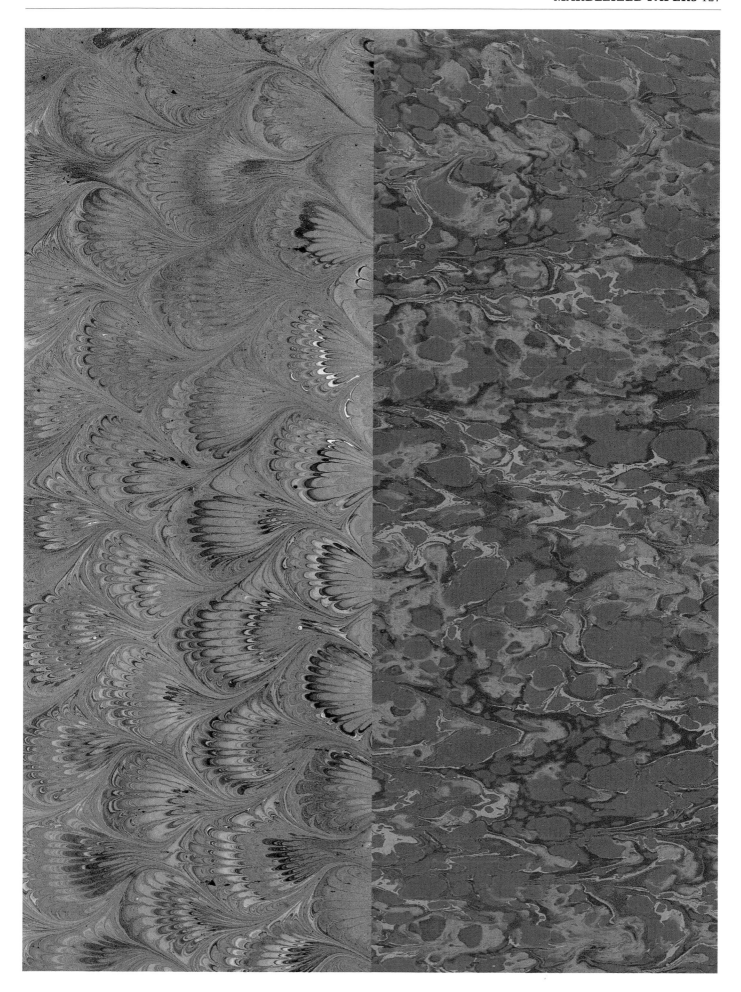

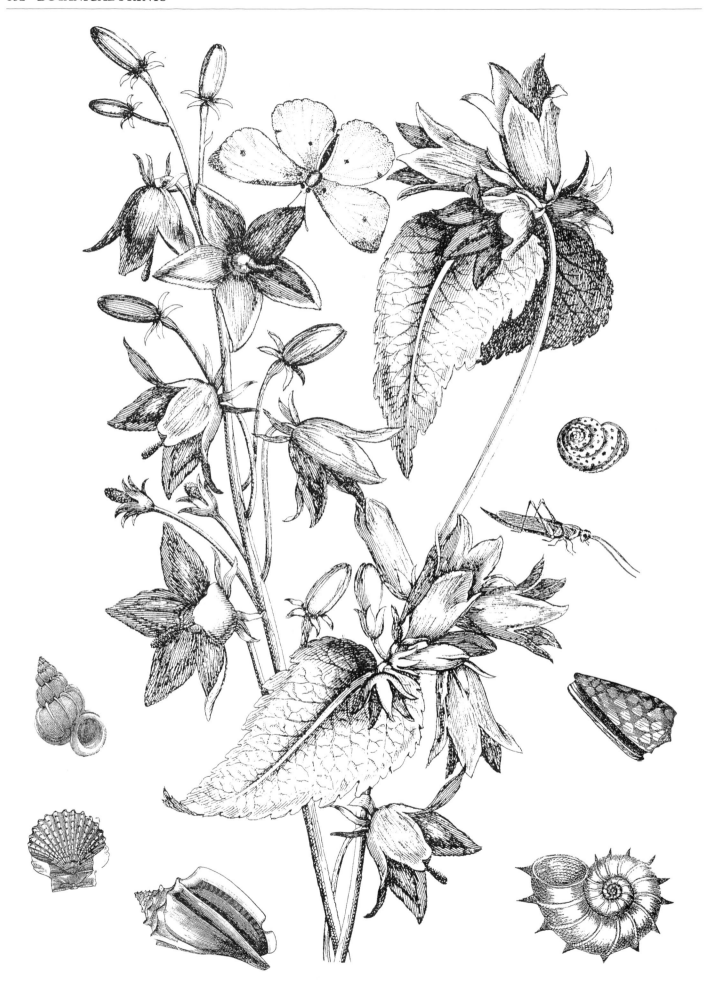

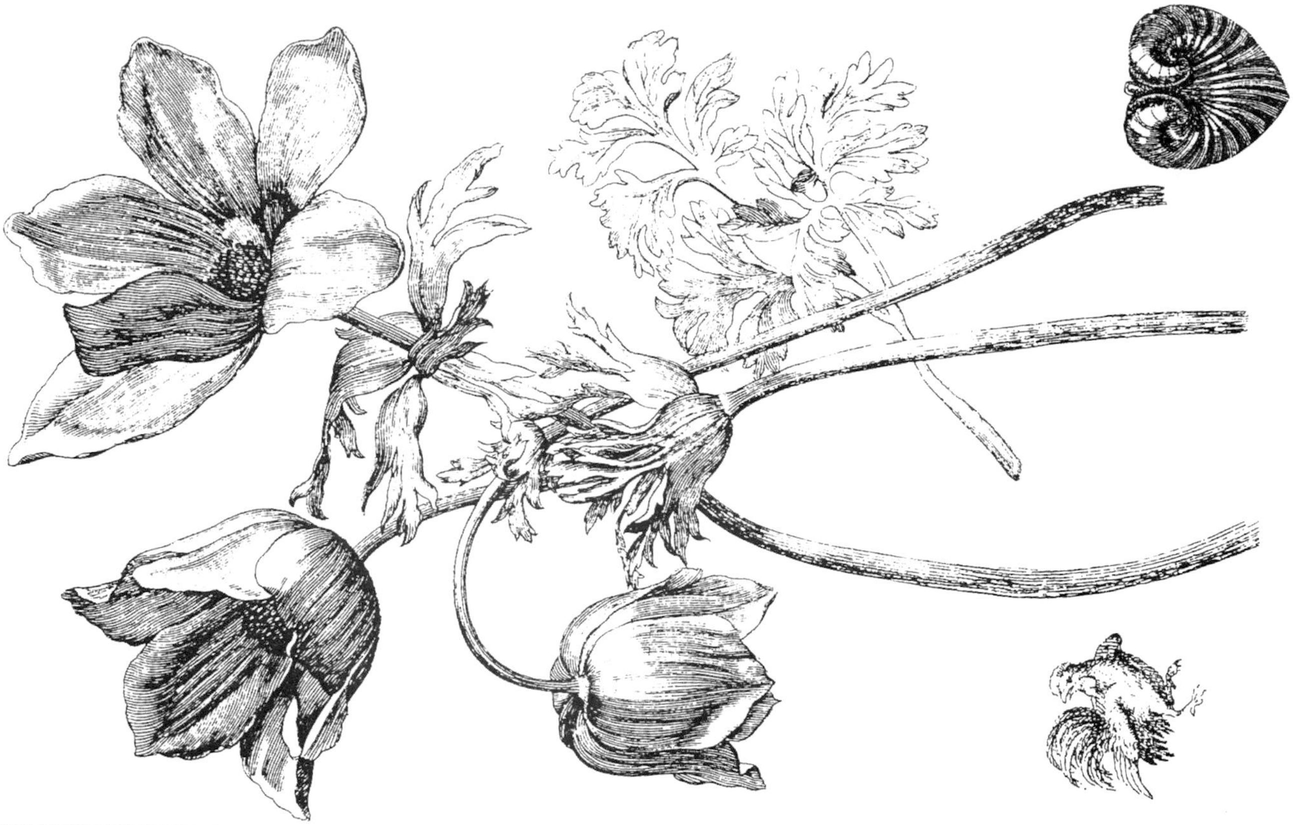

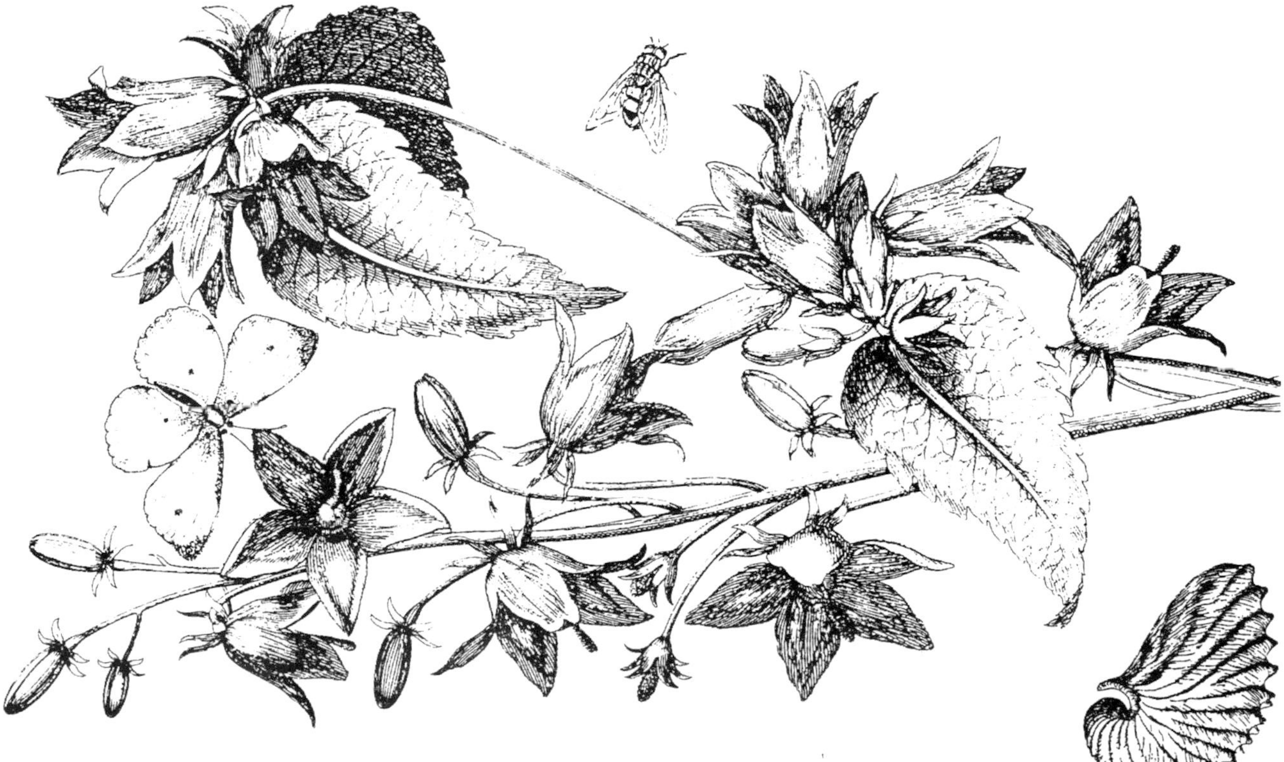

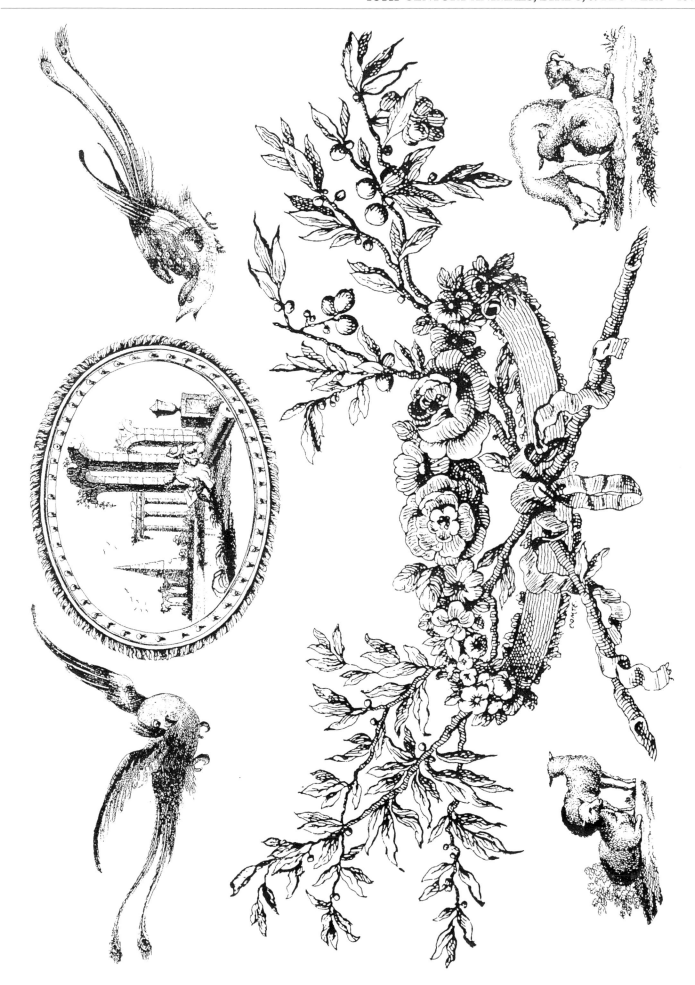

Grow old along with me!
The best is yet to be,
The last of life, for which
the first was made:
Robert Browning

Mide y combina el tiempo y el sonido.

CANTO I.

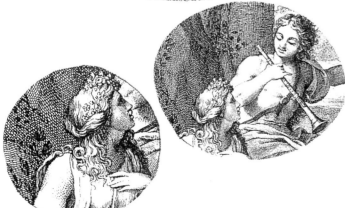

Mas ¿quién como la Música suave
De expresar las internas sensaciones,
Y moverlas tambien, el arte sabe?

CANTO II.

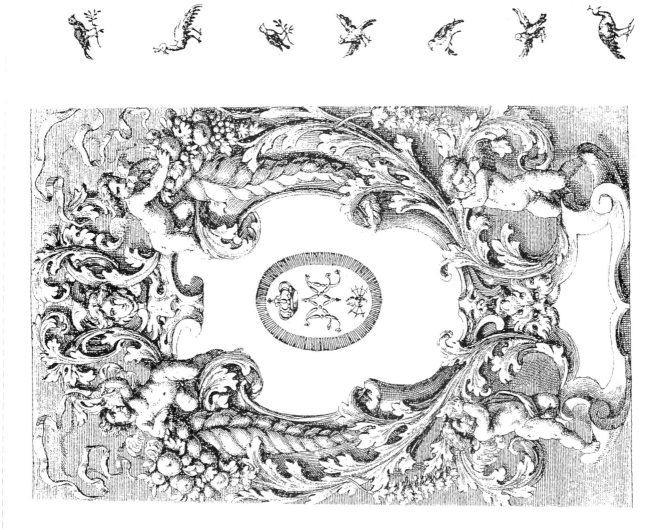

·CCXXIV·

·CCXXV·

·CCXXVI·

·CCXXVII·

Gen. XLI. V. 42.

Gondôle Ordinaire.

Ex Museo Mastrillio

Io. Cassini inc.

Neapoli apud Teatinos

CCXXI.

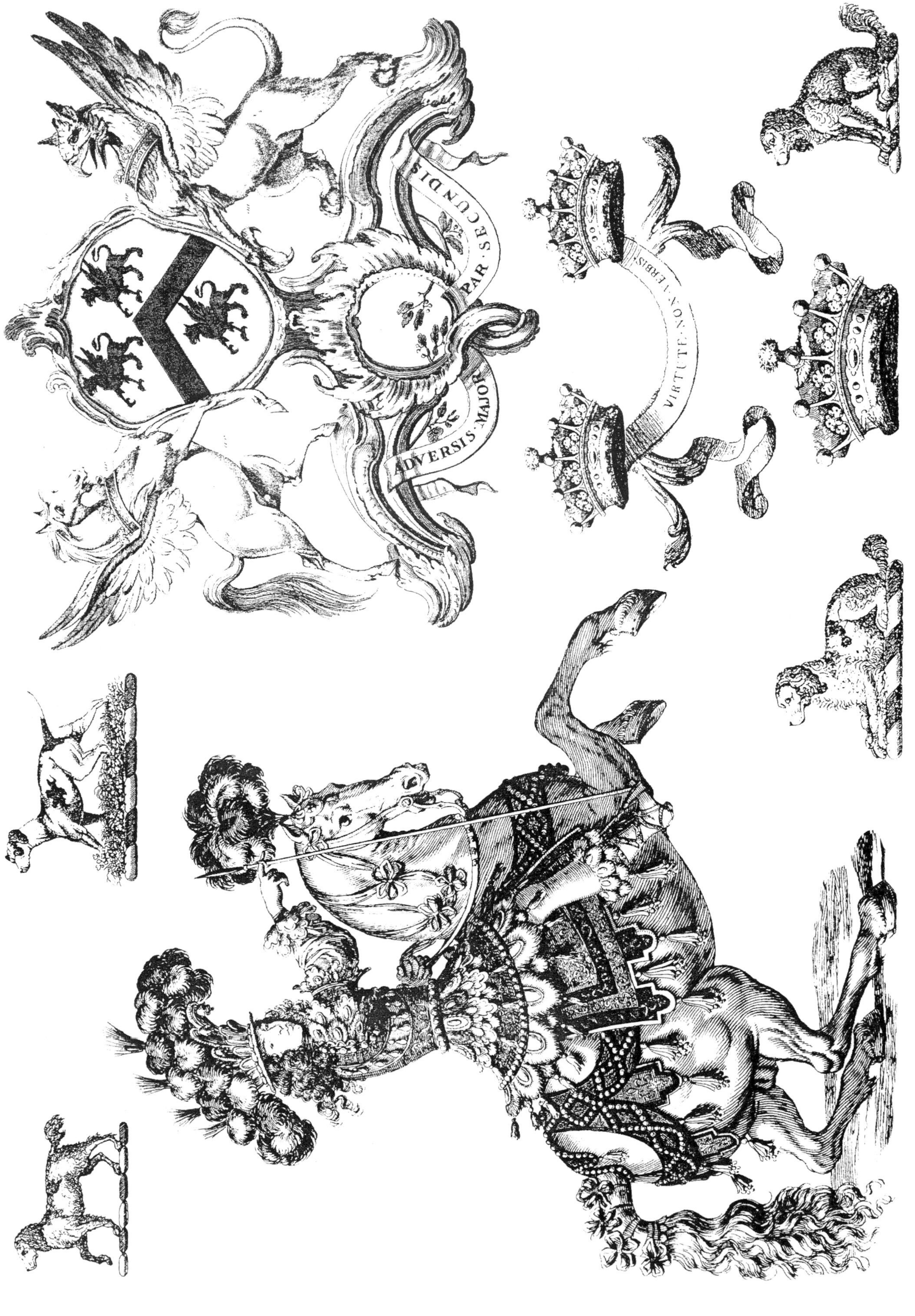
ADVERSIS MAJOR PAR SECUNDIS
VIRTUTE NON VERBIS

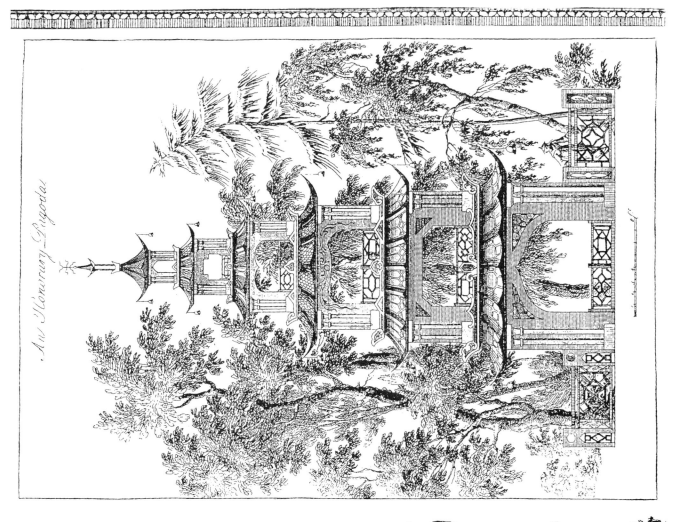

An Honorary Pagoda.

Garden Temple.

Umbrella'd Seat.

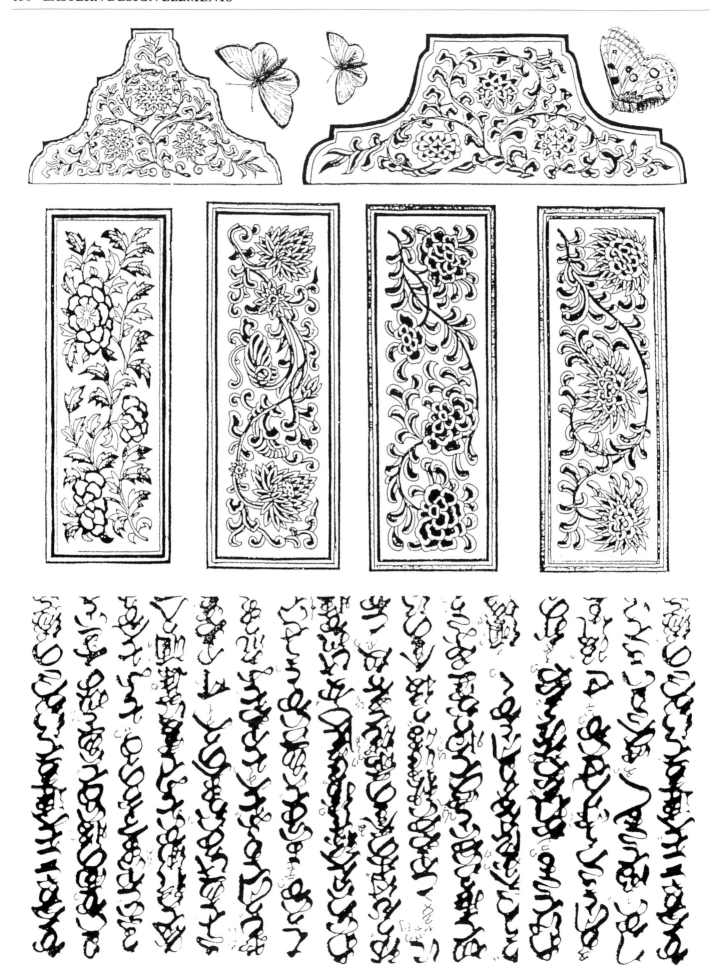

HARPER'S WEEKLY.

AUGUST 26, 1865.]

PARIS FASHIONS FOR AUGUST, 1865.

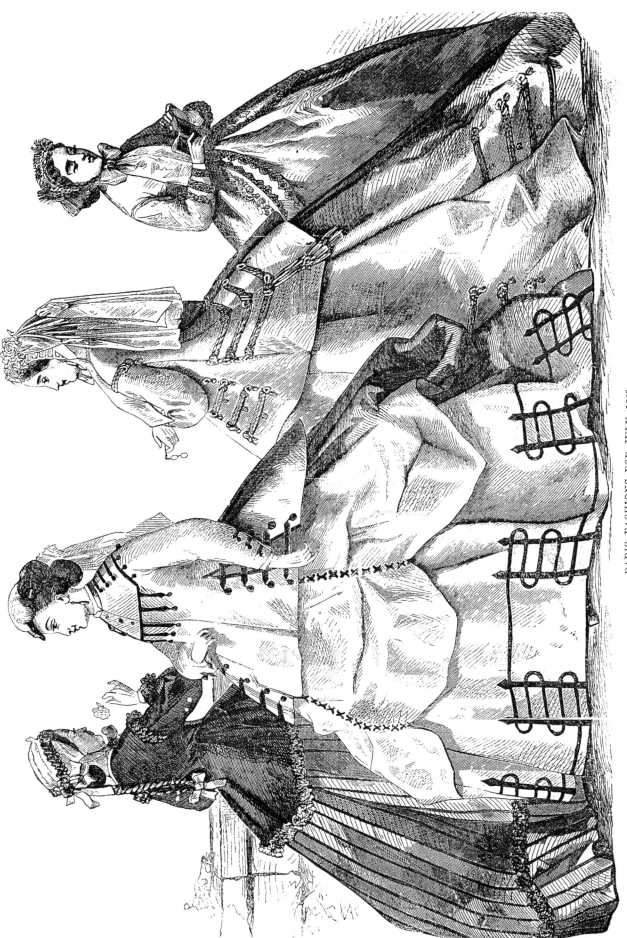

PARIS FASHIONS FOR JULY, 1865.

PARIS FASHIONS FOR OCTOBER, 1865.

PARIS FASHIONS FOR SEPTEMBER, 1865.

"Without music life would be a mistake."

這下子，左右前後車廂裡的人全圍上來看熱鬧，車掌也來問究竟，要看她的護照。結論「原來您是美國人啊！」此時她如自覺不太妙，暴露了身份。結果在後來的幾天幾夜只得緊緊的抱住她的皮包，上上下下的硬舖去廁所，也不敢睡得太熟。因此一到了南京，當然就兩倒了，又是感冒又是拉肚子。

幸虧南京方面的朋友，幫她弄到抗生素，她才痊癒。當然，我們在太平洋的這一邊乾著急，打了不少長途電話。那一個月光打到中國大陸來的長途電話就花了美金六百元。（後來從大陸來的朋友告訴我，在火車站臨時想買車票等車幾乎不太可能的）。

然後，純如又請了南京當地嚮導帶她勘查這各處日軍當年大屠殺時斬首、槍斃國軍的刑場，這些地點，據她說多半在南京城外荒涼雜草叢生之處。純如在南京的八月天，烈陽下，汗流浹背的在野草高過人頭的荊地來回徘徊憑弔，直到夕陽西下。夜晚回到旅館，發現身上被蚊子咬了一身紅塊，癢得無法入睡。

我這個媽媽又在這邊焦急萬分，立刻打電話到美國舊金山美國傳染病治中心詢問，及由電腦資訊網上查詢世界當時瘧疾、腦炎猖獗之處。幸好南京當時並沒有瘧疾及腦炎流行，但真也讓我們心痛不已。當她在南京時，又發生了一件國際大新聞。在美居住的吳達又弘達又偷渡入境時，故查獲逮捕入獄。當時，中美關係吃緊，我們擔心純如她的安全。因為那時，美國人特別是美國的記者作家，是不太受歡迎的。像這類敏感的事，我們愛在心裡，是無法在此描述的。不過我們很很佩服她的勇氣。

在華盛頓找到原始資料

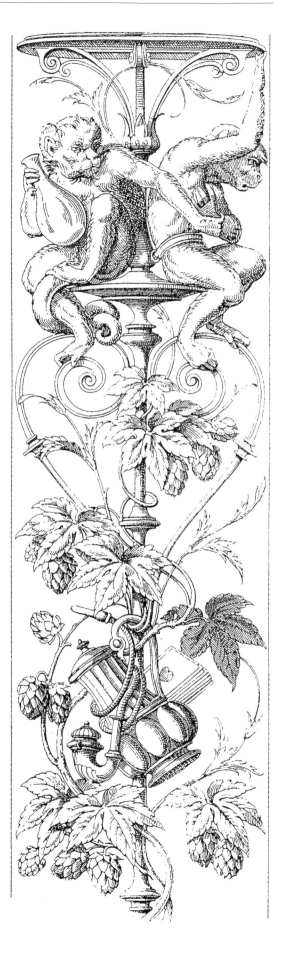

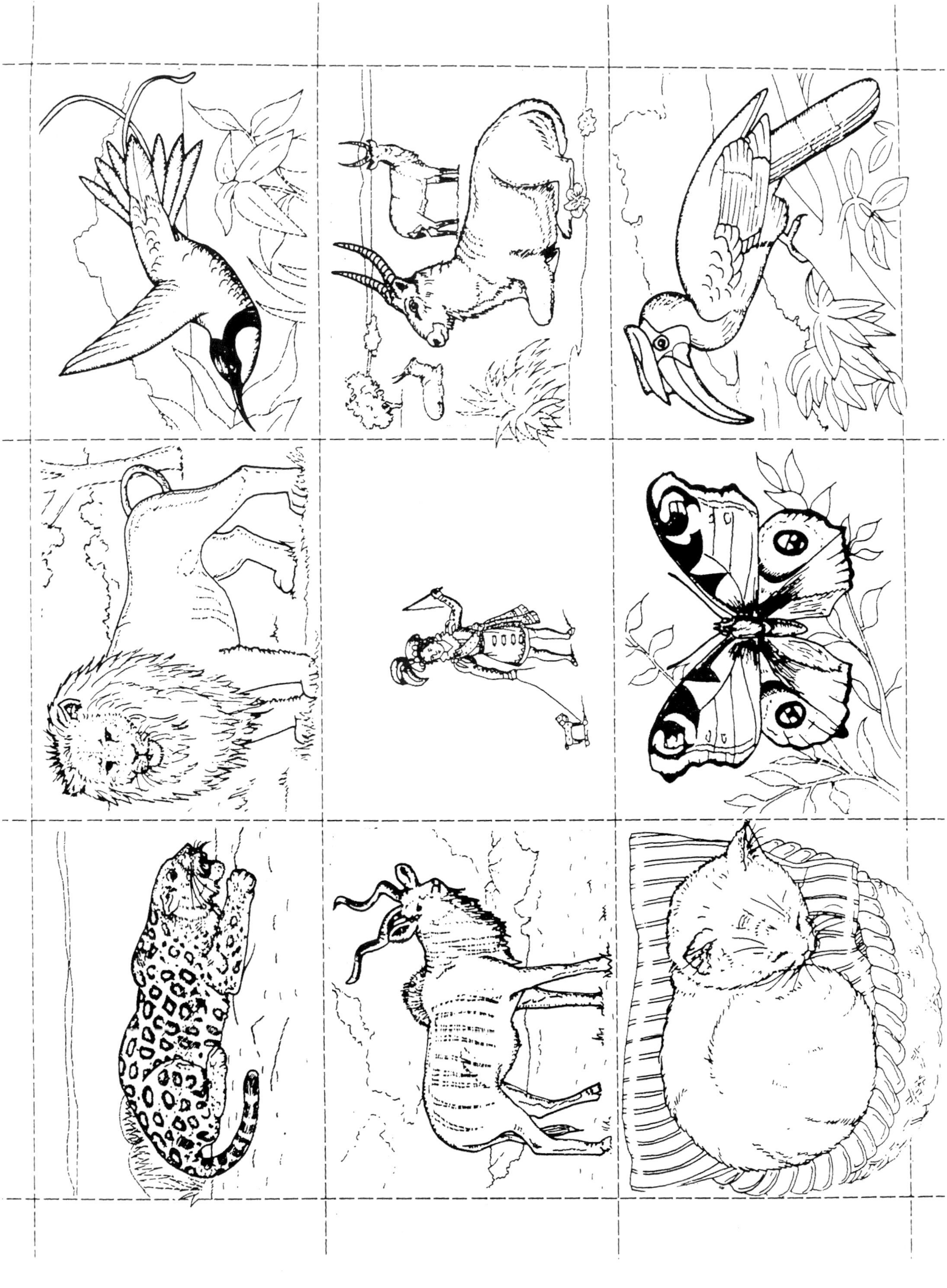

REDINGTONS NEW FOOT SOLDIERS

N.º 5.

London, Published by J. REDINGTON, 73, Hoxton Street, Formerly called 208, Hoxton Old Town.

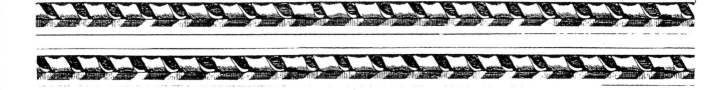

A B C a b c

A was an Acorn, that grew on the oak ;
B is a Boy, who delights in his book.
C is a Canister, holds mamma's teas ;
D is a Drum, you may sound if you please.

D E F G d e f g

E is an Eagle, that soars very high ;
F is a Fox, that is crafty and sly.

H I J h i j

G is a Griffin, of him pray take heed ;
H is a Hare, that can run with great speed.
J is a Judge, that the law oft obeys ;

K L M k l m

K is a Key, that no secret betrays.
L is a Lamb, often frisks o'er the lea ;
M is a Mermaid, that sings in the sea.

N is a Nightingale, dwells in a wood ;
O is an Ox, whose beef roasted is good.

N O P Q n o p q

P is a Peach, that did grow very high ;
Q is a Quince, makes a savoury pie.

R S T r s t

R is a Raven, rapacity charms ;
S shining Sun, is the Banbury Arms.

U V W u v w

T is a Trumpet, your merit to raise ;
V is a Vulture, on other birds preys.
W a Wren, that was perch'd on a spray ;

X Y Z x y z

X was King Xerxes, well known in his day.
Y is a Yew Tree, both slender and tall ;
Z Zachariah, the last of them all.

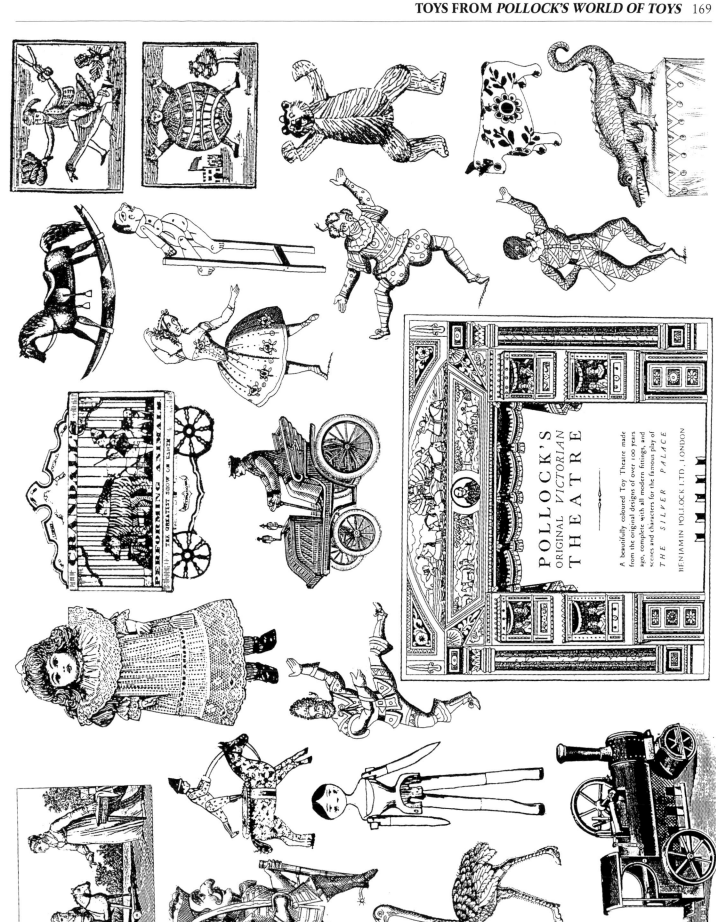

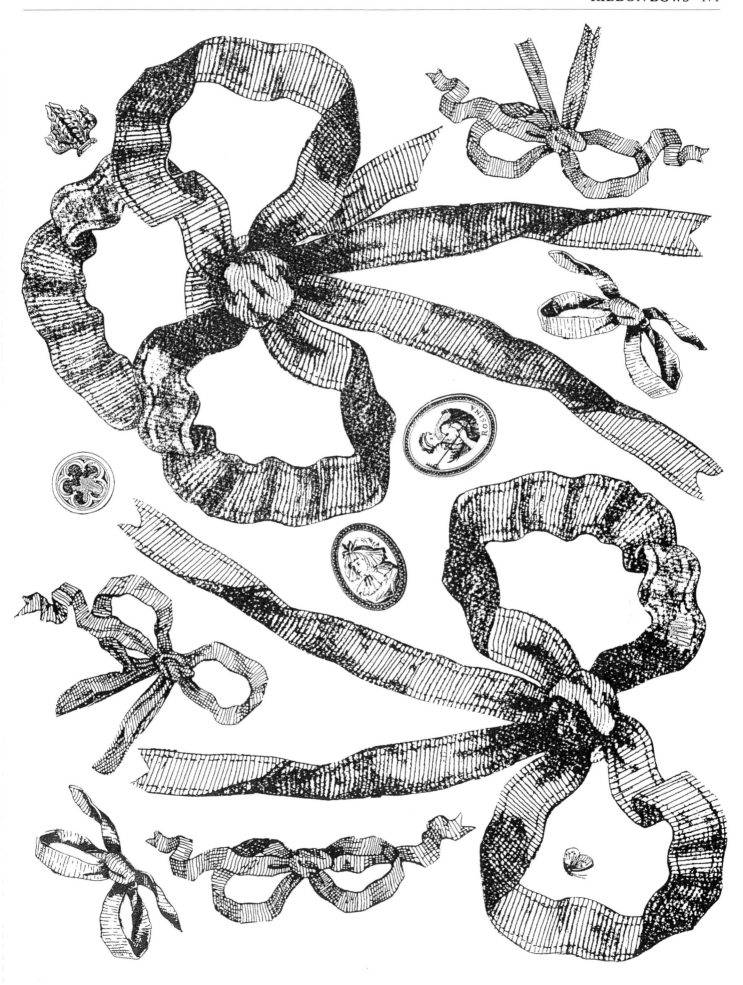

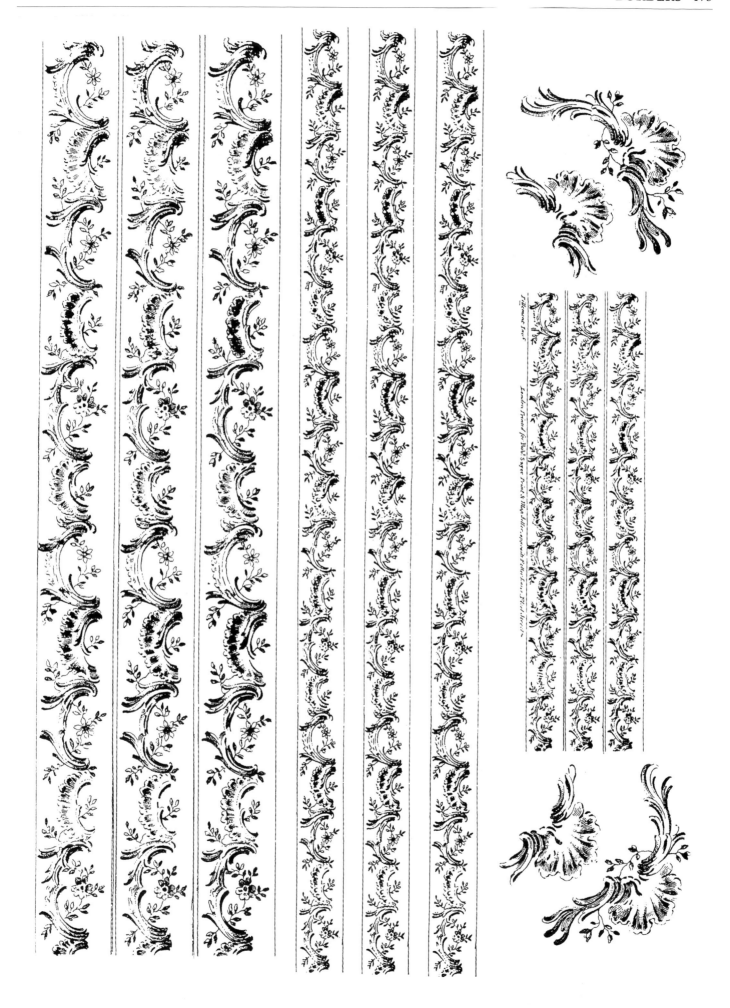

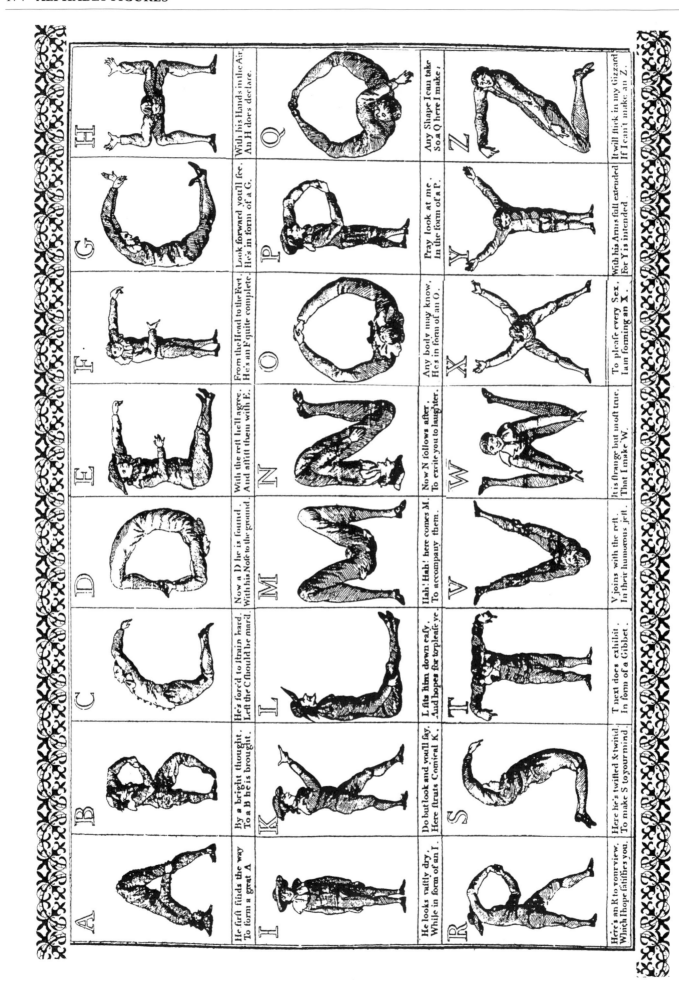

RESOURCES

The following are useful sources of decoupage materials and other art supplies. Note that some suppliers charge a small amount for their catalogs.

Adventures in Crafts Studio
P.O. Box 6058
Yorkville Station
New York, NY 10128
ph: (212) 410-9793
Specializes in decoupage tools, materials, books, kits, wood boxes and accessories, many shown in the photos in this book. Has a mail-order catalog.

Back Street
3905 Steve Reynolds Boulevard
Norcross, GA 30093
ph: (770) 381-7373
Manufacturers of paints, finishes, books, papers, and kits. Specializes in "scheren-schnitte" (silhouettes).

Daniel Smith
4150 First Avenue South
Seattle, WA 98124-5568
Seattle store: (206) 223-9599
catalog: (800)-426-6740
Both a mail-order catalog and a retail store with a few locations in Washington state, Daniel Smith offers all sorts of art and craft supplies, including papers, glue, paint, gum arabic, and much more.

Kate's Paperie
561 Broadway
New York, NY 10012
ph: (212) 941-9816
This store, one of three Kate's Paperie locations in New York City, offers a wealth of beautiful papers, including stationary and wrapping papers, and paper-related projects, such as handmade journals. Catalog available.

Pearl Paint
308 Canal Street
New York, NY 10013
ph: (212) 431-7932
toll free: (800) 451-7327
Possibly the world's largest art, craft and graphic supplies center, Pearl often offers discount prices. You'll probably be able to find many of the supplies that you'll need here. Pearl has retail stores in California, Florida, Georgia, Illinois, Maryland, Massachusetts, New York, New Jersey, Texas, and Virginia. You can also call to request a catalog.

Plaid Enterprises
3225 Westech Drive
Norcross, GA 30092
ph: (678) 291-8100
toll free: (800) 392-8673
Manufactures paints, finishes, books, and kits. Catalog available.

SUGGESTED READING

Davis, Dee. *Decoupage: A Practical Guide to the Art of Decorating Surfaces with Paper Cutouts.* London: Thames and Hudson, 2000.

Grotz, George. *The Furniture Doctor: A Guide to the Care, Repair and Refinishing of Furniture.* New York: Doubleday, 1989.

Leland, Nita, and Virginia L. Williams. *Creative Collage Techniques.* Cincinnati: North Light Books, 1994.

Pearce, Amanda. *The Crafters' Complete Guide to Collage.* New York: Watson-Guptill Publications, 1997.

INDEX